The Lion Addresses the Wild

Dedication:

This book is dedicated to: GVZB, WEBIII, SRB, JRB, the lovely NDB, KZB, and JDB. For shaping the life that informed the meaning of my words.

Cover Art by: Kyrie Bantom
Cover Art Illustration by: Jaden Bantom

Author's Note:

I truly believe that poetry is the conscious act of painting the subconscious. My hope is that where your mind goes while reading is where healing/joy/reflection/imagination wanted more color.

These are offerings from my journey to yours. I wish you fantastic painting. - gB

Order:

Sometimes the good…1
was/is…2
Hand me down…3
Awkward of mouth…4
Cottage…5
From a storm that has not formed…7
Loopstick Bramblebush…8
Guess at honor…13
I live in my neighbor's house…14
Today worked all day…16
New Moon…17
Days that start at night…20
becomes a habit…30
honestly…37
this film is not yet rated…38
BGM…44
Writing is the admission I can form words…48
piggy bank…49
more, oR LESS…54
slip…65
One, Nothing…66
Whole Notes…70
Score…71
Those black and white photos…77
I don't even do my job…78
What the pot called the kettle…82
The headache you can't hear…85
The Club…90
does dies…91
How to edit a letter…92
History kinda…98
Open Ended…99
Do you think we own birds…101

Museum of the Altar…102
what I wrote told me…106
The Boy Along The Way…107
I am Not a Diagonal Man…113
Infinite Small Talk…116
Relating to the Radius of Realization…123
And when you get really stuck…125
Maze. …126
Soul Knows…128
The Lion Addresses the Wild…132

Sometimes
The good
We experience
Clarifies
The obstacles
We manifested

was/is

I was raised in a den of fragile badgers
I moved on
When those that taught me to run
Could no longer keep up
So I got a few things going for myself
And a few holding me back
I try to paint from memory
Though I was told
I had the wrong impression
I meet a lot of people
Whose eyes follow me
When out of frame
Of their self-portraits
It never occurred to me
That my pattern
Had been corrupted
Until tension erupted
To totally interrupt it
And we will all soon recover
What these long nights
Have learned
From our most productive days

I live my truth

However it is
And whatever it was
Every today
I am another chance

hand me down

there is a fruit
too ripe to eat
rotting beneath the sun
obsessed with both stages
of living and dying
of feeding and poisoning
of helping and hurting
questioning it's flavor
for a taste of approval
and at its core
is a seed
to start again
a fruit too ripe to eat
never in its prime

Awkward Of Mouth

Gee
I seem
To make myself
Confusing
That way
If you never
Choose me
I can
Pawn it off
On how
You never
Knew me
So when
I say
Excuse me
It is not
For scrutiny
Or a martyred
Pity me
I am just
Simply
Under construction
For being
Understood

Cottage

My home
Is protected by insecurity

Though
It only has one room
For storing jars of potential
That are being preserved
For sweet regret

Embarrassment
Spins webs in dark corners
For my gossamer confidence
To feel watched
From odd angles

And I sit cozy
By my windows with
A picture perfect view
Of the outside
That is almost
Too perfect

I project myself
Fitting in
Out there
Although
Somewhere
In this cottage
Is also a person
I want to be

From my lonely

Open windows
I find it difficult
To learn faith
Without
Familiar boundaries
Like trying
To know nature
While never leaving
My home base

This safe space
Is enough for me
Even when I feel
I cannot afford
To live here

No one will ever see
Where I live
If I do not see it
In myself

And I sit cozy
By my windows
In my cottage
Plain as day
Somewhat terrified
Anyone notices
That because I am
Never satisfied
I cannot recall
If I ever locked
My only lonely door

From a storm that has not formed

I am grounded by how
Healing is revealing to me
That allowing life
In waves
Means that stress
Is typically temporary
Whereas
I used to soak in
My worries
As evidence
That I had been living
A life
That always caught me
Drenched in trials
Which in turn
Triggered my anxiety
That I may never change
Now
When peace norms
As a disruptor
I allow it
To finish speaking
Since there is no forecast
Calling for
The echo of thunder
From a storm
That has not formed

Loopstick Bramblebush

I got lost
Running away
From my hidden desire
To grow up

Assigning origins
To the bumps
In my nights

Confidence
Only enhances
Follow through
So I kept it moving

Though
The only result
I commit to
On a daily basis
Is leisure

I am the man
According to
The boy that
I am

Telling the tall tale
Of how I fear
Growing out
Of all
That I grew up in

When the story
Of my surroundings
Do not honor
The grand legend
Of my ambitions

I retreat
At the very least
To be well regarded
In smalll circles

Incapable because
I easily get uncomfortable
In any container

I like the flow
My fragile ego
Knows

And there is a part of me
That has just become
So comfortably jaded
About achieving normality
That no longer feels
Anything
About the consensus
Image of success
And for a time
That hurt me
Because I saw art
In the crying
And the joy
Of finding a smile

So I laugh
When contrarians sigh
Because if not today
Tomorrow
Or thereafter
We will swear
We got our
Answer
About what exactly was
A Loopstick Bramblebush

I breathe
So I take up space
And the reasoning
To accept
What is presented
To me
happens naturally

Like that calm you get
When you watch rain
And feel forgiven

And we did not
Shake hands
Yet
Those are the terms
Of that agreement

I would know
You
In the dark
So do not make me
Say

All that I see
In myself

It already hurts
To know I was cared for
When deciphering
Loopstick Bramblebush
Annoyed me into
Indifference

And you may
Break your neck
Trying
To turn your back
On yourself

So I try to move on

But I bet you
It is based in higher learning

Like do popular people
casually know
Then act indifferent

Can a bramblebush
Even loopstick

Has anyone else listening
Even made the connection

Is it something familiar

Why does the unknown

Nag my conscience
With such
a passionate insistence

Because if I cannot
Sort out my confusion

Then what chance
Do I stand

With existence

guess at honor

Ordinary
Requires
So much
Effort
Only
To feel like
A sparsely
Attended
Surprise party
When it
Arrives

I live in my neighbor's house

I leave my actual house
And immediately
wonder who sees me
I walk taller
Vigilantly
Checking all angles
Like I am setting an imaginary alarm
Around my perimeter
I make commitments
To improve my vehicle
By shaking my head
At scratches and dirt accumulation
A nod to my commitment
Against becoming an eye sore

I truly live in my neighbor's house

When I go out
I capture everything
That tells my story
For a sold out audience
At a venue
That has yet to reveal itself
Complete with photos
Live videos
And more emojis
Than I have emotions
A nod to being liked

I truly live in my neighbors thoughts

I work extra hard

At the hard work
Of working
Complete with unhappy hours
Of co-worker monotony
With telling glances
To Camera B
A nod to the notion of a live studio audience

I truly live to be discovered

I come home
To a well-stocked
House of memories
Nostalgia puts on a running record
Of my greatest hits
That serves as sustenance
For an appetite
Impossible to fill
And my private desire
When I edit my due dates
And dispose of refuse
Is to be seen as the tidy neighbor
A nod to civil contributions

I truly address my identity
To those
In my immediate proximity
Until I can afford
A place of my own

today
worked all day
to give you tomorrow
perhaps
take the night
to think about that

New Moon

Bright
In the
Darkness

Perhaps
This is only
A phase

My childhood voice
Was lost to the ages
Although
The voice of my childhood
Stages
Most
Of my vulnerable acts
Before an audience
Full
Of quarter moons

Slim hopes
For a sliver
Of attention
Wash over
My tranquility

Not everything
Out of reach
Is above me

From my perspective
Family
Is a home with a hole in it

For the coming
And going
Of fluid emotions
So I tend to inspect
The integrity
Of any receptacle
Prior to pouring my heart out

Promises
Make compelling agendas
For surviving most nights

I was told
This was
Only a phase

If being fully present
Actually
Turned the tide
Then
Where would I
Expect to find
Passion
In water

Or
Would I be
Unfazed
To discover
Where water
Was in me
All along

Out of everything

Reaching
Above
Is within me

I must
Spare the myth
Of a final farewell

Bright
In the
Darkness

New Moon

Days that Start at Night

We all age
According to
The quality of
Our days
That start
At night

The high energy
Have to be
Convinced
Of the
Merits of
Rest

The
Overwhelmed
Seem to
Struggle
With
Feeling
Overburdened
By the hour

For the
Restless
And
Insomniacs
Discomfort
Is powerfully
Relentless

Perhaps

We call it
Evening
Because the day
Is balancing out

Sunsets
Setup
Sunrises
As the
Sun cycles

The high energy
Have to be
Convinced
Of the
Merits of
Rest

So if you
Do not
See me
Then
It is truly
Your
Night time

We are alive
The whole time
We are alive
Yet we
Find hours
Feeling empty
By being
Repeatedly

Inspired
And deprived
By our time
Spent reaching
For
Optimism
And despair

We must
Have blushed
At the idea of
Of naming
Time
While we
Made peace
With
Monotony

Anxiously
Over accounting
For the
Weighty moments
Between
Our extremes
While
Attempting
To experience
Enough life
For all
Of our days
That start
At night

Sunsets

See
Nights awaken

The
Overwhelmed
Seem to
Struggle
With
Feeling
Overburdened
By the hour

If the sun
Did not peak
Would a week
Still hold
Deadlines

Perhaps we
First felt
Progress
When we
Named
A day
Mine

My version
Of Faith
Is a lack of
shame

You cannot
Tell me how to
Construct

My building
While I am
A work
In progress

You cannot
Tell my story
From some
Ancient tome

As far as
I know
I have only
Scribbled
A prologue
To the places
I will go

No
The journey
Is my home

Every tall tale
Bound
To orbit
Completes
A loop

The beautiful
Compromise
Of remaining
Alive
Is the view
Of the many

New
Days
That start
At night

Sure as
Sunrise
Days will
Also sleep

For the
Restless
And
Insomniacs
Discomfort
Is powerfully
Relentless

At some moment
We were all sleeping
At some moment
We were all blinking
If even for a moment
We all closed our eyes
To clear our minds

While
Base needs
Daily
Demand duties
For the meek
The night
Neatly
Encourages

Abandon

Some people
Savor
The sweet
Serenade
Of solitude

Star light
Star bright
Can you
Build me up
In the dark
Of night

A semi-selfish
Communication
To trace
My blueprints
From the
Outline
Of these
Grand
Constellations

This is
The struggle
Of designing
While occupying
My days
That start
At night

Sun Cycles

We will live in our time

Perhaps
We call it
Evening
Because the day
Is balancing out

When the
Biorhythm
Repeats
We
Track
How
Stopping
Prolongs
Going

I used to be
About numbers
Until I learned
To count
On myself

Extract my soul
From the clock
Tick back
My timing

What
Will I do
With a day

Days

Do not return
They become unique
In memory
In breathing them

When we began
Counting them
They became antiques

When we begin
Counting on them

We repeat
Days
That start
At night
Just to
Justify why
Rest assured
We manipulate
Our feet
To
Come outside
And play
With
What we
Will never
Forget

That old
Faith
Informs
Fate
To look

Past the
Perception
Of a tipping point
Where we see
Our lives
As solely
Cynically
Switching sides
In the hour glass

Magnifying our
Comings
And goings

So
Waking up
From sleeping
With memories
For dreaming
Keeps proving

Our days
In fact
Start at night

Good evening

becomes a habit

Your habits
Are metaphysical
Fences
Fortifying
And defining
Your
Personality

You gotta
Imagine
A box
A normal box

All of the sides
Exact measurements
And parameters

Now think
In and
Outside
Of the box

A box like
Your head
Imagine
Your brain
Wrinkles and all
Thinking inside
And outside
Of natural
Walls

When you lock
A door
Is it the ritual
That compels you
Or is it what
You imagine
Is now outside
Reasoning
Propelling
Justification
Are you ever
Secure
Inside
Your behavior

Stand
On your back
Or simply lie
On your feet

Sometimes
Systems
Of self-soothing
Surface
Idiosyncrasies
So subtle
We scarcely
Subjectively
Claim their
Significance

Personal patterns
Peripherally enhance
Personality procedures

What do we call
This dance

You gotta wonder
If this
Normal box
Can handle
The force
Of holding
Your
Living

Not all tendencies
Are unproductive
Indeed some
Are generally
Understood
As good

Expending our
Energy
Eventually
Leads to
Entropy
Therefore
We sleep
And
During these cycles
DNA replicates
To keep making you
You

Relentless
Replication

Right on time
We all do it
Although
Try applying
Normal
To people
And you make
Fewer friends

Is the act
Of being social
A natural trend
Or a familiar
Forced function
To see which
Spaces
Our DNA
Fits in

You gotta form
A familiar box
Bound to
Delivering relief
Folding in comfort
As a possession
An asset
Set up
To repeat

You gotta ask
Is this a bad
Box

Bite a nail

Build a home
Throw a party
Live alone

Responsibility
Is not included
As a requirement
In maturation
So what you do
And how you do it
Heavily impugns
Your compass
For successful
Navigations

Is anxiety
A habit
Can peace
Become one
Whichever
You are lacking
If you cannot
Physically have it
Can you release
The stress over
Your reactions
To grab it

When we
Cannot
Get a hold
Habits
Help us
Grow old

Or die hard

Whether
Wanting
Or winning
We can get
Boxed in
A behavior
Either
Hard to break
Or desiring
To be undone
As if
We are asking
Our DNA
Over
And over
If I do this
Or if I do not
What will I
Become

The nervous tick
Emerging
From the conundrum
Of determining
A worthy
Living
Outcome
And how to
Align solid goals
To enjoy life
As one
Of one

In any case
The function of
Owning
Your own impulses
Makes you
Beautifully
Tough to
Break

Consciously
Or not
We present
Our bodies
But rarely
To hide
Or seek
So please
Be gentle
With your
Habits
For they are
Your spirit
Attempting
To speak

Outside
Of the
Box

honestly

my truth
is not true
for everyone

we may share
the air
but my story
speaks to me

this film is not yet rated

I could always
See myself
Up there

So
When I wanted
To grow up
Faster
My imagination cast
My ego
As a stand-in
Slash stuntman
Crashing
Into
Personalities
Take
After
Take
Until directed
To cut
And get
Back to
One

Where I finally
Got the note
To stand in
My light

I have been
Trying
To find my mark

From the moment
I became
Head of
My own studio

My actions always
Held up
Several people
Around me
Although
I still cannot
Edit
When I fade
To Black

So
I work
To be seen
Despite
Hearing
Horror stories
Of how
Huge
Celebrity status
Sells out
Reality

I am aware
That you are
Watching
Though
I rarely
See
My own work

Sound is
Always
Rolling
On set
Ups
For special screenings
Of
Inner visions
As in
Film festivals
Moving pictures
For all audiences

Which actually
Ruins
Continuity

So
After
Several
Re-writes
And stoppages
Of
Production
My crew remain
Professional
Primarily
Because
I am bound
To tell this story
The way
It was meant
To be told

To remain
Relevant
I tease
Plot points
Though
I am still
Running
Lines
From my
Trailer

This film
May not
Be suitable
For all
Audiences

I spend hours
In the writer's room
Procrastinating
And
Perusing
Coming Attractions
Lest my
Log line
Leaks
And I become
Redundant
Or resembling
A remake
Rehashing
The original
Just to reminisce

Around
How I
Don't
Make me
Like I used to

Any more
Sequels
And the franchise
Loses me
As EP
To some
Indie project
Simply for
The authenticity

This film
Is not yet
Slated
For post
Production

My DP
Doesn't believe
In schedules

So the call sheet
Changes
Daily
Depending
On
New locales
I scout
For the climax

My manager
Supports the contract
Extensions
My agent sees
Conflicts
As booking
Preventions

I just wanted
To see myself
In the
Big picture

There's no business
Like my fit
To finish
My story

So
This film
Is

BGM
(background music)

I grew up from
8 bit elated to
High def deflated

The sweet distractions in life while I was hard at work with the living task

When I first played
Video games
I never went into options screens
Once I did
And I saw
Three little letters
BGM
as a setting

And I thought
What does bgm
really mean?

Doing your homework should teach
you that we are conditioned
To sit and think through our problems
The sweet sound of distraction
Proves how often we make time
To not solve them

Square peg circle hole
Rough around the edges

There is no perfect.

And that's just perfect.

As long as time wasn't running out
BGM played on a loop

The circle works to complete itself

I have the tendency to believe what I hear
Because I know what I'm listening for

A lullaby as an alibi
For time gone by

And I get lost
and thought
Where would I be
if I were looking for me
And almost immediately
Thought how disturbed
I could be
If I did not instantly know
Where I should be
And I get lost

Even as the focal point of my journey's side scrolling screen

With the flickering lamp
of fading determination in the eyes
Resourcefulness is prized
When life plans are eaten alive

Initial scores of comparison offer
A lullaby as an alibi
For time gone by

When the heartbeat of existence
Became the background music
And the miracle of life
Lost out in priority to improvements
New toys
New wars
Changed skin
New more
PC sin
Motherboards overloaded
Rising import on
Holy success being decoded
Three worlds
on one orb
The programming is bloated
Control one man
Understand
How the Boss Level
Got so lonely

Digital Glory is far from phony
It's what we spend our coin on
Dismantle a motive
For all its components
And the picture remaining
Is no turn on

For when did we start
Depicting ugly in art
Was that also
A shift in existence
And for the child at heart
Blank paper a chart

To egress obligation's insistence
Sometimes we're fine
Outside the lines where
Authentic self-acquaintance
Reverses the versus life current
Just as the ominous
Countdown to tears
Serenades the
Human ear
With a deep cut
From the sequence
Of a fear
To continue
The code to
compete with
One's self

BGM
Background music
Pursuits ensue for stages to win
Instead of levels of truth

Only one life left
Thoughts on how to use it
Play on my conscience
Sweet background music

Writing is the admission
That I can group a bunch of
Used words
To try and explain myself
Yet the stories
I cannot cease thinking about
Keep forming gangs
And revolting

piggy bank

Poverty

Inserted
Intentionally -
Into
Force fed
Food chains -
Baked into
Cognitive
Deficits -
Serves
Predisposed
Notions
Of desperation -
Making sense
Of hunger -
Keep eating piggy -
Prior to
Perception
Pulling together
Principles
Of speech -
Nouns got
Named as
Artificially flavored
Verbs -
For the
Purpose
Of cramming
People
Places
& Things

Down the consumer's
Throat -
Inward
Investments -
Inserted
Intentionally -
Ingested
In dire
Circumstances -
Seconds
Into another course
Of fiduciary confusion -
Keep eating piggy -
Piggy please
Do not break -
Bracing for
Gaps stuck
In the teeth
Of starvation -
With limited means
You pick at
Understanding -
You feed
With your hands -
Keep eating piggy -
Pull the string
Of an open market
And the properties
Prance about
By the push and pull
Of puppeteers -
Mimicking
Real human movements -
Lips do not move

When old
Wooden
Characters
Sing anthems of
Living traditions -
Stumping us
With rings
Around
White collars -
We never
See
The work -
This is a knot
I am untangling
That was
Inserted
Intentionally -
Why don't you
Move piggy
Do you not know
That money is alive -
Is saving
Taboo for you -
Or a pattern of
Pleasant
Performance
Anxiety -
Piggy
Is saving
Money a lie -
Manipulating
Our logic
To one day
Appear

Permanently content -
Greed can wear
A survivor's mask
Never letting you pass
With enough in your grasp -
Rather taxing
To unpack
Who gets
To break the glass
While the well to do
Stock up laughs -
Unplugging your
Stash -
Shaking out
All you have -
To make ends
Last -
It is sickening
How the well-fed
Get fat -
While those
With literal piggy banks
Are starving
For scraps -
And how despair gets
Intentionally
Inserted
Into
Reflexes and
Instincts -
Testing me
Digesting me -
In
Bloated

Systems
Sick with
Bulimic empathy -
Ceremonially
& clandestinely
Burping up
Laws
To consume
More order -
Stuff your piggy face piggy -
Regurgitating
Manners
In proper
Fashion -
Piggies
Banking on
Saving
Sloppy seconds -
Slotted for
Scraping
Together -
Leftover

Wealth

more oR LESS

Is need worth
The price
Of admission

Need
Talks
About itself
In the third person

And will
Remain hidden
Until
Called upon

Would I buy
That need
Is me

this little bully
Went to market
This little bear
Stayed home
This little squirrel
Stashed acorns
And dogs
Eating dogs
Break bones

Dangerously
Desperate
Debt ceilings
Demand

Natural
Resources
So we corner
The market
On sticks
And stones

More or less

I sound like
Greed
And look like
Assets
I burn like
Fire
Yet I
Remain distant
As the sunset

I began
As an
Impulse
Fostering
Civilizations
An
Imperceptible
Addiction
A glutton
Tortured
By
Starvation

More needs
Haunt you

To have
Less

Oh
How need values
Values

It does
Not matter
What we do
When soaked
In the residue
Of financial faith
It is
The commercial price
Of comfort
That sees us
Lick the plate

Give
Or
Take
The need
To
Domesticate

Try to
Family
Without me
To love
Without
A mutual
Loan
Try

Incorporating
Your independence
Try
Squeezing into
A salaried scenario
Without me
And see if
Blood
Does not
Come from
That stone
I push
That rock
Into your
Hard place
Deal with me
Or live
Alone

Would you buy
That need
Was also greed

Even though
Need
Generously
Disappears
Into what
Becomes
A career
How can
Labor
Be greedy
With what

It makes
In a year

Socially
I am
Legally tender
Globally
I am a
Loquacious
Wallflower
Tying up
The conversation
Through
My conception
Of commerce
As exclusive
Storage bins
Easily manipulated
By an
Overstock
Of commodities
Disguised
As businesses
Dissected on
A butcher block
Into synthetic
Cuts of
Capital
Bound to
Go bad
Which is
Only good
For those
Who can

Make sense
Of this trade
But I am only
A wallflower
So you did not
Heed that
From me

Less needs more

Algorithms
Tell me
I am only
As stable
As a robust
Portfolio
And
I know
You are
But what
Am I

Did you
Forget
Who we were
Talking about

Need I
Remind you

Would you buy
That need
Turns your screws

Investing me
Manifests you
Save space
So I can
Follow you

From every
Breath
To every
Follicle

Coveting
Every living
Molecule

Cause you
Are already
Too
Worried
Which
Worry
Would
Follow you
To
Your grave

Does this
Ring a bell

For
Fear
Of self
Worth
Will never

Offer you
What you
Need
Nor
Will it
Stop you
From buying
Your way free
Of debt
To me

And I
Need that
Information

Spend
Your life
Doing what
Currency does
Changing
Hands
While your
Values
Suffer

And oh
How need values
Values

More or less

Because the
Sheep see
The flock

Whereas the
Wolves
See
Each other

less as more

Before you
Attempt
To have it all
Please know
That accepting
Loneliness
Is an inherent
Code
For finding
Flaws

Would I buy
That need
Is also meek

Would I
Need to
Tip the scales
In my favor
If I overheard
From a neighbor
Regarding
Another neighbor
That my grass
Is a dull green
Compared
To the

Landscape
Of their
Endeavors

I need
A future
To credit
My past
That leverages
My physical
As long as
I can last

Although
In my mind
I need
Months to
Years
To unveil
My mental
Mirror
And heal
My mending
Self-love

More is more

Perhaps less so
Than the greater
I too need
Selfishness
To tax
Me later
So I can

See
If any
Of my
Thoughts
Are worth
Your price
Of admission

Because need
Presupposes
Permission
And charges
Morals
The commission
To be an
Upstanding
Global
Citizen
Unless I
Can take
Time
From
Your needs
While you
Pay
Attention

More or less

Slip

And when that mountain
Inverts into a pit
Apply your skills
To where you stand
On this shared land
Try and climb back
For you
Are everyone again
Just be careful
We all slip

One, Nothing

A resistance
To rock bottom
As a starting place
For renewal

How zero
Factors into
Your healing
As an
Energy level

Everyone has a limit
But who is keeping score

Please avoid
Being rigid
While learning
Yours

If knowledge flow
Was meant to appease ego
We would only ever learn
What we already know
About ourselves

Your people
Pleasing pipeline
Is over populated
With persons
Not named you

Aaaanyhouse
Knock knock
What's next

You have to
Hold you
Differently
For the
Punch line
To take effect

For
The things
That do
Get in
Take a lot
When they
Leave

The setup
Was never
Due to
Aptitude
Or
A love
That speaks
In apologies
While
Finding familiarity

What was your
Favorite zero

That stretched

Your timeline
For experiences
From positive
To negative

To teach your
Inner-child

Something about
Standing up
To cowardice
And not burdening
Every journey
With a
Massive load
Of happenings
Deconstructing
The practicality
In why
The chicken
Crossed
The road

In the wild
It only takes
Thirty seconds
For the
Predators
To find the
Prey

Finding familiarity
Is deja vu
Consciousness

Conceiving
The whole
Of time
Commenting to
The soul
Perceived
As you

I do not know
How to hold on
Though
In the swirling
Everything
I cannot
Let go

Sanity
Has a limit
But patience
Is keeping
Score

One

Nothing

Whole Notes

Only
Innate
Musicians
Can be lost
In a melody
And also
Sonically
Everywhere
At once

Score

How can you
Write a note
And trust
Anyone
To hear it
The way
You do

Now
I can keep the time
I held my head
And screamed
Pain into silence
As a likely overture
Waking
The weight
Of
Masculine
Supposings
And puffed out
Bravado
Staccato
Pounding holes
In my modeled
Role
Of standing up
Lightheaded
In the
Intervals of
Ritualistic
Resignation
A worn down

Refusal
To quit
Playing along
I hear
The drumming
In my ears
Left over
Legato
Right after
Crying
Reflexively
Asphyxiating
Rhythmically
As my chest
Finds pain
In snorting back
The complete
Loss of faculties
From the opus
Of my leaking orbs
The melody inquires
How I can trust
That you hear
The pit
Of my stomach
Relentlessly
Clenching intestines
In the same manner
As some possessive body
Downplaying
Convulsions
Through
These notes
That were

Never mine
To sing myself
Calm
When
The ringing
Dead flesh
Of fist skin
Reanimates
Pens
And needles
Mere seconds
After punching
Walls to force
The angst
In flat tones
Away from
My body
Ejecting
The hope
That this vessel
As a major work
Would sustain
The attention
Of an audience
Playing the note
For you
In the same space
As my
Broken breathing
And mucus strained throat
Nothing
Is more
Innocent
Than sound already is

And this
Confirms
The false
Harmony
Of hatred
Negating
The dull duty
Duly appointed to
Pride
To crescendo
Holding out on
An end to
The mechanics
Of bravery
Conducting
Percussive
Sharp shallow
Pains in the heart
In the symbolically
Cleft thrombosis
As a major artery
Glissandos
Panic
Known
By the neck hairs
As a movement
Externally provoked

Rest

And you're telling me
An evocative note
Can be named
To express

This pain

Rest

And you
Now claim
To know
How
I am
Meant
To be composed

Rest

For those
Who hear
My non ivory key
Anxiety
As playing
Out of tune

What is
The score

Does
The meter
Adequately
Capture
The reader

Full
Rest

For

How can I
Write a Black note
And trust
Anyone
To hear it
The way that
I do

Those black and white photos
From library books
Have reappeared
In color
Outside my window
Prompting fresh looks

I don't even do my job

I paused
On my way to school
And the curiosity
Of what my parents
Did for work
Caused me
To follow them
And guess what
All the adults
In my family
Went to build
A bridge
All ages
All body types
The hard work
A bridge
Stemming
From the dark
And intentionally
Neglected
Broken parts
Of the city
Where I lived
Yet here comes
The unbelievable
And the uncanny
By the end of the day
All of my people
Had completed
Their day jobs
As well as working
On this bridge

I got tired
From the weight
Of that reality
I slept
Under the bridge
Many nights
To eavesdrop
On the conversations
To decipher
The laughter
From the jokes
That were funny
To the chuckles
About the people
Who were funny
To the silence
That spoke
All languages
And required
No translation
In this way
The bridge extended
And I became
So engrossed
That I started
To mimic the workers
My family at first
Then my neighbors
My friends
My community
And what I learned
Were skills
Inherent
In my people

Talent
And intelligence
That often
Superseded
What I saw
In a world
That called
Us their own names
Here at the bridge
The raw
And uncultivated
Uncharted
Personas
Reserved
Their most
Sincere efforts
For bridge work
While possessing
Capabilities
To construct
Fully functional
Careers
Contributing
To work
Away from the bridge
Full Artists
Full Teachers
Full Doctors
Full Contingent Workers
Full Employees
Fully capable
And
What that did
For me

And in me
When I felt less than full
Was to inspire
Completion
In my work ethic
To put in
The extra effort
And history
Tells me
There is so much
Bridge left
To construct
So perhaps
You did not
Run into me at work
Perhaps I was there
And you looked right past me
Perhaps you thought
You were speaking
For me
Or to me
But I was busy
And that's because
I didn't do my job today

I did two jobs
With my full self

What the pot called the kettle

Tip of the cap
To the design

A tea kettle
Capitalizes
On a reaction
In a confined space

Fill the container
Do other things
Make other plans
The boiling begins

One less task
To worry about
Since all of the ranges
Matter

Tip of the cap
To the design

It is of no concern
If the contents splatter
Pushing themselves
While fighting for space
Boiling over in agony
Reacting
To inherited catastrophe
Pressure applied
Constantly magnified
Forced into
Realizing their place

The kettle was made
To shield the eyes
From the volatile combustions
Brewing inside
During this time
We may question why
But in the course
Of a day
With more important mouths
To feed
Who
From outside the kettle
Questions chemistry

Tip of the cap
To the design

The irony in response
From outside the kettle
Is typically rooted
In inconvenience

To respond in frustration
To whistle blowing exclamations
And yell at the kettle
For even making proclamations
Honestly the kettle
Should be happy
To be owned

Then ask the poor kettle
While controlling the heat

To ask the abused kettle
Exhausted in defeat

To blame the poor kettle
While rinsing to repeat

This intentional crucible
At the tipping point
Full of compressed steam
Shrieking into space

Why it made
Such a commotion

Then engage
This judgement
In silent speculation
About how
The kettle
Can very easily
Be replaced

You have got to love
The design

The Headache You Can't Hear

The smile you can't hide
The vibe you co-wrote
The tableau you create
The energy you emote

An acquired
Taste
For a couture
Space

A sip of the irresistible
Paired with a shot
At localized
Immortality
Affirmed in a dap

Spoken in lyrics
You enshrine
Into a night
Composed
Of melanated skin
And all that smoke
Against

The headache you can't hear

Eye lines are highways
Where heartache
Jams traffic
And heart break
Rushes hours
Into collisions

Of synchronizing
Coordinates
For selfabrations
Of stunting
Alignment

Boogeymen
Apparitions
Simps
And pacifists
The superstitious
Speaking to
The blasphemous
Over a chorus of
Passages
Razing a silence
Needed to
Express
The commotion
As locomotion
For how the night
Remains
Alive
For

The headache you can't hear

A Lithe
Slide by
From the
Apple of your
Side eye
Pantomiming
How you

Could neva
Even though
You cute
Or whateva
And all the feels
For

The headache you can't hear

Coming
Home
Owes me nothing

For showing up
And showing out
Are what growth
Are all about
For
What endured
At the roots
Blossoms
At the
Leaves

And still
Owes me nothing

Coming home
Is visiting
What invested
In my youth
And now
Recoups
The prize

My heart
Can barely
Believe
My eyes
This yard
Of my
Youth

Owes me nothing

And so
The headache you can't hear
Is the world away
From here
From this oasis
Pounding
On your socializations
To return

So before you step away
You time stamp
Your memories
With the smile
You can't hide

For on those facial creases
Extending
From your wild heart
Of belonging
To a community
Viewed as
Another planet
Yet right

Behind your house
Is the true you

Surviving
Anonymity
As
Black
Excellence

The vibe you co-wrote
The tableau you create
The energy you emote

Even
As I move
My heart
Knows
My place

The Club

Some people
Are mainly
An accumulation
Of the last thing
They heard
Other people
Desired

Good luck
Getting
Out of
That club

does dies
with a slip
of the i

How to edit a letter

Dear inner voice,

I keep trying
With communication
Hoping
It is my turn
To be understood

Where to begin
Perhaps
A letter
To myself

Well if that letter is
I

Then really
There is
No real way
To be a human
Hence
Understanding
And assimilation
Are really
All I has

Unless I
And
Other people
Can be
Incomplete sentences
As we organize

The predicate
To make
Our verbs
A statement

And if I
Could be
Abstract
And paint
Self-portraits
Where the
Metaphor
Of my forehead
Was a blank page
And my brain
Was a cloud
With a pencil
Sensing storms
And sunshine
From my heart
I would
Share how
Whether I
Was ready or not
The elements
Still
Move in me
To influence
My story

Inner voice
Shall I
Present myself
As a lower case

Just to keep
The point
Over
My head

As a child
i established
Myself
By being irrational
When the history
Of manners and grace
Would audit
My actions
I clung to my
Absurdity
To take up
Space

Without a
Socially
Acceptable
Name
I was known
By my
Utility
In a
System
Of shame

For there is no
Source of truth
More potent
Than what you
Believe

In a moment

How much
Could I
Pay
Attention

The truly
Selfish
Build a shell
Of those
Tolerant
Of their
Torture

My insecurities
Would not allow
My vanity
Not to be
Haute Couture

Dearest inner voice

I
Am the only one
That knows
The through line
Of my story
So I draft pressure
From peers
To distinguish
Those who integrate
My presence
As a major influence

In their chapters
From those
Who regard me
As a footnote
To a hypothesis
They were proving
To themselves

Blank margins
Hold space
To frame
My content in
Stationary
Boundaries
So I can
Write
Freely

Well if that letter
Is I

The most beguiling
Function
Of giving anything
Living a name
Is the false idea that
Each time
You call it
It will be the same

I edit change
And that
Changes me
To either become

A better denier
A better liar
Or a
Better letter
Writer
With a signature
That inspires
The reader
To admire
Yours
Truly

History
Kinda needs
Something living
To make it
Exist

Open ended

Your fate
Is being who you are

Your fate
In that sense
Has already been decided
Your destiny
Is based solely
On your destinations
And this is fluid
As we change directions
Constantly

We often assign
Fate to tragedies
And
Destiny to successes
However this thinking
Stems from our need
To justify outcomes

The beautiful reality
Is that all realities
Are eagerly awaiting
Realization

Release from
Patterns
Creates freedom
From expectations

A good question

Is the strongest tool
For dismantling
What your soul
Wants to rebuild

Do you think we own birds
Do they fly
Like they know us

Museum of the Altar

Eyes closed
Grand opening
Pay what you can
Feel something
But please do not look away
Experience the self
From excruciating angles
Only bad sides
On display
Exhibit A
So life like
How the purple of deep bruises
Echoes freshness
My pain
Swollen lacerated
Skin hides everything the canvas'
Bloody disdain
With closed eyes you cannot blink
So there is no refrain
And you try to look away
Though the pupils from every self-portrait
Scream in your brain
Seeing what you remember
And what it means to echo pain
Exhibit Two
Every stroke of genius
Drenched in bitter feelings
Depicting tragically broken hearts
And how you're words
For loved ones
Came out so profane
But you cannot look away

For when the skin is drawn over
And dust receives a gust of air
You recall
Your naked body
This judgmental world
The comparisons
Depleting self-care
There is no flashing allowed
Through echoes of deep pain
Exhibit Three
How laughter
Frustrates the senses
Pointing fingers
Teasing out your sanity
A hunting party
Captured timelessly
Chasing some classic game
Please turn off all defenses
And look at what you've done
To trick the eye in any portrait
Establish a zenith
In an infinite sustain
Of embarrassed emotion
But you simply must not look away
A lack of catching breath
Tantamount
To painting a pitch black night
In the blended hues of regret
A few brush strokes
From being right
Post-modern echoes of true pain
Exhibit You
Darkness approaches
Weak knees halt all steps

Sweaty palms
On velvet ropes
Please do not cross any lines
This memory is a collectible
Rare even for its kind
The self-loathing impeccable
The vulnerability sublime
Evoking a timeless inner dialogue
Either
Experience this work of art again
Or bargain with life's decline
Though you won't look away
Stomach twisted in knots
Words cannot save you
Skin cold
Blood hot
As if the artist knew
Why I get
What I got
I really want to look away
From echoes of knowing pain
I had convinced myself
This never happened
Yet here it is
Perfectly framed
And I learn not to look away
I need to understand
Yet
Why are all the placards blank
Where is the artist's name
Is this body of work
Just living here
Woefully unclaimed

For all this suffering to go unnoticed

That would be a shame

What I wrote told me
Listen close to your heartbeat
It serves as your ink

The Boy Along the Way
(for K&J)

The head is bowed
Long before
Making eye contact

Space in the womb

We are born
Affixed a personality
Firmly in place
A predicament
In that
We have yet
To escort
Our personalities
To lots of places

Requiring parents
Who are
Proficient
At play
To usher
Their
Progeny
To imagine
All potential
Possibilities
For
Progress

As innocence
Finds the egress

We digress
To daydreaming
With
Accountability
Can you
Clean your room
For
Improvement
With an
Allowance
For
Socializing
The goals
Of
The boy
Along
The way

As our fears
Become
Dear
To our
Circles
We grit
Our teeth
And brace
For the
Teenage years

Angst
Picks on
Anger
Picks at
Acne

Picks out
Anonymity
Picks up
Adoration
Picks apart
Acceptance
Picked for
Achievements
For the boy
Along
The way

Survive
That stage
For the
Entree
Of a
World view
Forming
At the
Same time
As your
Brain

Dealing
With plenty
You enter
Your twenties
And nothing
And no one
Will be
The same
Have fun
With the gang

Or isolate
The pangs
Of identity
As your
Energy
And
Life plans
Feel
Perpetually
Incongruent
As you begin
The long
Goodbye
And being
Truant
To the lessons
That won
The day
From the boy
Along the way

Pain
Arrives
In
The joint
Along with
Self-doubt
And worry
As you
Begin to
Read ahead
Into the chapter
Of thirty

Young enough
To travel
Old enough
To enjoy home
From
Trying your hand
At a soirée
To traveling
Totally alone
Married
To your zone
As business
Is calling
Contorting
Your desires
To align
To cash flow
Stocking up
Your strategies
To own
The future
That once
Belonged
To the boy
Along the way

Here at forty
Is a different
Story
Not quite
Middle aged
We will not
Know
When we have

Crossed the hill
Until our later
Days

For expectations
And fading
Glory
You must
Have your own say
Endeavor to tell
Your tale
With integrity
And sincerity
As the man
You have become
Today
You will always
Have a role to play
And you must
Honor
Your voice
And adhere
To your
Well-earned
Wisdom
As the rewards
For having raised
The boy
Along the way

I am not a diagonal man.

My grandfather only knew his father
through a mirror
and that mirror was positioned
at just the right angle for me
to see myself in my great-grandfather
and in so looking
I know someone will look at me

And I hope
in nights
that I shine like the moon
inspiring a long daydream
of pondering
what gave the moon that right
to glow and absorb with its very surface

I exist because of Walter and Gayl

I am no diagonal man

I exist in more than your periphery

The deep need is not my depth

Raising my face to the sun
Is how I bow my head

I am no diagonal man

The fear of different cultures is the fear
of agreed upon behaviors
upheld by many

That may harm me

I am no diagonal man

I will not learn my seasons in one summer

Some of me will form later or not all

And the thing about pain
The longer I endure
The easier to accommodate

And I would still choose neither

I am no diagonal man

In clouds of civilization

I clean my own dishes
I wash my own clothes

More of a decision than a commitment

And all I need is a sip of a whisper
To hear the roaring sea

I am no diagonal man

There was a time when I flowed like the breeze
and what came easy to me
was to go along with where I was going
Before knowing my day like train stations
fixed

and using a schedule

And I have journeyed long enough to know
that when I arrive

in that mirror
positioned at just the right angle

I will not be seen as a diagonal man.

I am

no diagonal

man.

Infinite Small Talk

What did the
Wayward wanderer
Whisper
To the wallflower
If you want
To know
Stay close

Good
Old Fashioned
Eye Contact

All undone bow ties
And bourbons

Toasting evenings
For those of us here
Acquainted
With the horizon
Of our ambitions

You hear
The haptic sequences

All handshakes
And grip assessments

Stay close

Two grains
Of sand
May never

Come into
Contact again

Ancestors
Requiring answers
Add fuel
To our
Neighborly
Curiosities

No one interviews
Dust
But we gather
To gossip
About you
Hoarding
Your possessions

Humans
Being single-minded
About social hygiene
In the whole
Wide
World
Wild
World
Why
World

When everyone
Only knows
Their own
Life

We are all standing
In the center

Stay close

All crowds
And the proximate sensations
Of
Soul awareness

Energy
Is a language

Wisdom
Is a work
Of art

Nature
Is humans
Being

All instincts
And keen focus

Owls at sunrise
Staying up late

Stay close

To feed
The circle
Of life
Surrounding
Social standing

I cannot
Consume
My rest
However exhausting
It may seem
To remain
Interesting

Logically
Eating
And sleeping
Double down
On separate bets
All for high stakes
One shot
With two banks
My hunger
To be pleased
My thirst
To be thanked

How easily played
How very cliché

Humans
Being sold
On a pattern

Although
When order
Begets rules
New data
Becomes
A threat

Stay close

All the shushing
And ensuing eye contact

Sometimes
I was only
As smart
As the sensible
Thought
That slipped through
The moment
So I owe
Some of my survival
To being open
To suggestion

In the whole
Why world

Stay close

All gasping
And finish lines

If you knew
How long
I took to arrive
Would you
Have asked
For a ride
Or let me
Pass you by

Social
Competition
Conditions
Improvement

Training
To win over
Our future selves

So
What did the
Wallflower
Whisper back
To the wayward wanderer

My voice
Is what
I believe

All suppressed smiles
And second thoughts

My voice
Constructs
What my architect
Commissioned
Me to realize

I alone
Am alive

My voice
Through

My ages

In the
Ensemble of
Infinite
Small talk

Staying close

Relating to the radius of realization

Some loops
Are in fact
A coil
If observed
For their
Layered
Dimensionality
The idea of
Making sense
Is actually
An exercise
In value alignment
And unless
I can shift
Your paradigm
We will remain
Locked in
A loop
Depth is
A perception
That shallow
People
Need experience
To sense
Therefore
Before we
Recoil in offense
Getting on
The same level
Is a dance
To the rhythm
Of patience

That frequently
Cuts into
Our loops
Of intolerance
So maybe
Understanding
The radius
Of our realization
Disrupts
Our ignorance
Deconstructing
The context of
Our circumference
To build that
Radius bridge
We require
To appreciate
Our depth

And when you get really stuck
And all hope seems lost
You make little agreements
To pull yourself up

Maze.

Is it the kind that's all drawn out
or that I can walk around in
where I can't find myself
going backwards from the end
because I haven't gotten that far yet
If I feel confused
I can't lose

The line
from my path
back through homesick nights
and rough living
heartfelt laughter
and ungrateful thanksgivings
my infested manifestations
and soothing daydreaming
I have too many memories to shed

The line
from my wrong turns
will be re-traced
if I don't make a mark
going forward
If I feel confused
I can't lose pieces of myself
all about

how those pieces
were intended to validate my progress should I choose to
return to myself
but instead
they fall out

Growing the grass that's greener
on the other side of the game
seeking the solace
that's hiding from me
and If I feel confused
about my profound fear
of being unafraid
Of escapes' tantalizing fame
and fortunate moments
that provide me occasion
to take my very breath away
before I encounter a dead end
and feel nothing
about my wonderful
and authentic
innocence
from my starting line
Is it the kind that's all drawn out
or a solution of mine
for the way that wisdom confirms
that I'm finding myself
just fine

line

between feeling accomplished

or being lost

in all
a maze meant.

Soul Knows

How does one
Contain
Such complexity

As celestial nomads
We have done
Well
For ourselves

At some point
It settles in
That what we are doing
Is
What we
Wanted to do

Bodies
Consuming time
Eating good

Though
The soul
Neither has food
Nor a diet

Yet there is a lot
To digest

Regarding our fitness
For existence

How does one

Count
In
Space

Lessons create
Ladders in our lives
Propped against principles
Constantly in peril
Of falling
Into a perception
Of fate

Curiosity
Is for
Sturdy faith

Questions
Negate
The concept
Of
Comfort
As we ponder
The circumstances of
Whom gets
Granted
Good fortune

Two things
We all get to be
Are
Dead
And
Wrong
Hence living right

Requires work
On
Revealing
What makes us
Feel alive

Crafting the story
Of what
The soul knows

In this way
life
Is a sentence

In a larger
Body
Of being

The heart
Is beating
The brain
Is thinking

So how is
One
Soul
Allowed to
Behold
All of
What we know

Living
Souls
Flow

From all
Of our sources
Of taking and giving

Simply stated
Self-discovery
Is the
Essence
Of

Knowing
One
Soul

In a larger
Body
Of being

the lion address the Wild

I begin by addressing
My appetite
For that seems
To be
A subject
Of some concern

The piquant taste of
Prestige

It is not
The steady state
Of wild animals
To take in
Other animals
By healthy means

I too
Have suffered
The caustic
Cackling
Of hateful
Hyenas
Hence
I age
With my
Wounds

So I roar
On occasion
Just to keep

The mane thing
The main thing

In this way
The wild
Learns
My name

It is not as much
That our extremes
Have established
A food chain
As it is
That our
Sense of place
Protects it

Preserved
For our
Nature
Even when
We know
Any animal
May attack us
It helps
To sleep
With a story
Surrounding
Our behavior

The messy taste of
Maturation

Fitting in

Outfitted me
With a Pride
I had never
Known

And
It is so
Challenging
To impress
Upon your offspring
Your goal
Of raising
A whole soul
Especially when
Your most
Consistent
Offerings
Are your own
Unrealized goals

And I know this
Because every day
The wild
Stalks me
For growing
Old enough
To know better

These are
The high stakes
Of nature
To remain
On the verge
Of knowing

Who you are

The savory taste of
Survival

For years
I was a
Problem statement
Penned
Down
By society
A cautionary
Consequence
Reinforcing
Romantic notions
Of domestication
Besides
What use
Have you
For a king

It became
A big game
To claim me
Thus reducing
My instincts
To the land
I made home
I had become
A reactionary
Fraction
Living on
My last nerve
Until I felt

New sensations
While hunting
New limitations
And found myself
Wandering
Off the reserves

Hence
I am
Now
Speaking
With you

So as
To not
Inherit
Worry
As a
Currency

I claw
Through
My self doubt
To remain
True

The gratifying taste of
Gratitude

I consume
What I hope
To lead

No one

Is obligated
To appease
My hypocrisy

What use
Have you
For a king

Ever since
I learned
That fighting
Was survival
I have
Pulled for
My inner child
To inspire
A revival
For I see
That little
Fighter in me
Braving the wild
Beyond the
Recitals
Of might
For space
And titles
Whilst clinging
To the belief
That my life
Is worthwhile

And as I
Preside
Over my

Future
And cool
My temper
In the
Tranquility
Of
Civility
Within
My soul
I address
My ambitions
And ask
My nature

What use
Have you
For a king

If the lion
Will always tame
The wild

Made in the USA
Las Vegas, NV
27 August 2025

27019995R00090